A SMALL GIRL

PEG AND MEG

THE MINISTER

3

SCENE ONE

In a town street, Peg and Meg are sitting doing nothing.

Narrator: Once upon a time, two women called Peg and Meg lived in a big town. They were always thinking of ways to make a lot of money. But they did not want to do a lot of work.

Peg: Our emperor is the richest man in this town.

Meg: He spends most of his money on clothes. He has different clothes for every day.

Peg: Every hour, more like it. I wish we could sell him some clothes. But we can't even weave.

Meg: That may not matter. I have an idea.

The Emperor's New Clothes

A PLAY BASED ON A STORY BY HANS CHRISTIAN ANDERSEN

Retold by Robina Beckles Willson

Illustrated by Doug Roy

THE CHARACTERS

THE NARRATOR

THE EMPEROR

2

SCENE TWO

At the door of the emperor's palace. Two guards are standing by the entrance. Peg and Meg arrive. The minister opens the door.

Narrator: Peg and Meg arrive at the emperor's palace.

Peg: Good morning. We are Peg and Meg. We need to speak to the emperor's minister.

Minister: That's me. What can I do for you?

Meg: We want to speak to the emperor.

Minister: He is very busy at the moment, changing his clothes. Perhaps I can help. Come this way.

Peg and Meg go through the door into a large waiting room.

Peg: We need to speak to the emperor because we are weavers. We weave the best cloth in all the world.

Minister: I will ask the emperor if he has time to speak to you.

Peg: I hope he will come, Meg.

Emperor enters.

Meg: Look! Here he is!

Minister: These are the two weavers, Peg and Meg, Your Majesty.

Emperor: I can't see any cloth. What can you show me?

2ND FLOOR · Emperor's 400 Closets

1ST FLOOR · Emperor's 100 Bedrooms

GROUND FLOOR · Kitchen, Throne & Government

BASEMENT · Dungeons

Peg: If you give us the money to buy golden silk thread we can weave special cloth for you.

Meg: It will be very beautiful.

Peg: But it will also tell you who is foolish and who is very clever.

Minister: What cloth could do that?

Meg: Our cloth can do that because it is invisible to people who are foolish.

Emperor: You mean they just can't see it?

Peg: Yes, Your Majesty.

Emperor: Of course, I know that *I* am not foolish. In fact, I am very clever. But it might help me to know who is foolish. And who is *not* clever.

Meg: I'm sure it would be very useful, Your Majesty.

Peg: So, would you like us to weave you some of our special cloth?

Meg: And make you a new suit?

Emperor: Yes, at once. Minister, see that Peg and Meg have all they need.

14

SCENE THREE

Inside Peg and Meg's workshop. They are showing the minister how they weave the invisible cloth.

Narrator: The two women asked for a lot of silk and gold thread, as well as money. They set up their loom and began to weave. But they were only pretending. The loom was empty, and the thread was left in its bags.

Soon the emperor sent his minister to see how they were doing. The minister did not see any cloth, but he did not want to seem foolish, so he said nothing.

SCENE FOUR

Inside the palace throne room.

Minister: Peg and Meg are working hard, and the cloth is beautiful.

Emperor: I must see it for myself. Have it brought here at once.

Minister: Right away, Your Majesty. Everyone in the town has heard about this special cloth. They are longing to see it.

Minister leaves quickly.

Minister enters with Peg and Meg.

Emperor: Now, is THIS my cloth?

Meg: Yes, Your Majesty. Isn't it beautiful?

Peg: I hope you like the colour.

Emperor: Yes, of course I do.

He is not sure.

Narrator: The emperor did not really see any cloth, but he did not want to seem foolish, so he said nothing.

Minister: You must have the suit ready for the procession tomorrow.

Meg: We will have to work all night!

Peg: But we are glad to do that for Your Majesty. I will cut out the suit at once.

SCENE FIVE

At the workshop of Peg and Meg.

Narrator: The next day, the emperor and his minister went to see the weavers.

Peg: This suit is so light, it will seem as if you are wearing almost nothing. Would you like to try it on over by the big mirror?

Meg: Then we can help you put on your new suit.

Peg: And this beautiful new cloak. You will need two people to walk behind you, carrying it.

Meg: Do the trousers fit, Your Majesty?

Peg: And the jacket?

Emperor: Yes, yes. But it is a cold day to go walking in a procession.

Minister: A lot of people are waiting to see you.

Emperor: Of course, they always like seeing my new clothes.

SCENE SIX
᷉

The procession through town. The emperor is walking along wearing only his underwear.

Narrator: The emperor was at the head of the procession. Everyone said that his new clothes were beautiful. Nobody wanted to say they could not see his clothes. They did not want to seem foolish, or not clever. But . . .

Girl: Look, Mum! The emperor is in his underwear!

Peg, Meg and Minister: Ssh!

Girl: But, Mum, he's only wearing his underwear!

Peg, Meg and Minister: Ssh!

Girl: Why is the emperor only wearing his underwear, Mum?

Peg, Meg and Minister: Ssh!

Narrator: The emperor heard the girl, and then he heard everyone quietly agree that he only had his underwear on. All he could do was keep walking, with his head held high. He felt very cold and very foolish.